THE STORY OF THE CHEROKEE PEOPLE

by
THOMAS BRYAN UNDERWOOD
illustrations
by
JACOB ANCHUTIN

Contents

ISBN 0-935741-01-1

I   In Ancient Times

In the vast silent pine forests of northern Siberia, roamed tribes of men, who lived on the berries and fruits of summer plus the coarse raw meat of the mammoth and prehistoric buffalo. They hunted the buffalo and mammoth with spear throwers and hand spears and lived in houses made of their skins. They followed the herds of mammoth, much as a sheep herder follows his sheep, taking what animals they needed for food and letting the others continue their eternal wandering through the forests and over the grassland. This was from thirty to forty thousand years ago.

Before the dying of the last great ice age, a land bridge existed between what is now Russia and Alaska. The tremendous amount of ice and snow which built up during the ice age caused the seas to recede and leave this land bridge. Across this low lying plain wandered many tribes that eventually became the American Indians. Unknowing and unheralded, they drifted into a new world.

The migrations across the land strip continued at intervals until the sea rose up and covered the passage. Even after the passage became covered, other migrations continued.

Gradually, as more and more tribes of wandering hunters came to the new land, they spread south and west and began to prosper. In Asia, the getting of food and clothing had been a most difficult task that let only the strongest survive but in the new land, game was plentiful and the winters not as bitter as in former times. Son begat son and not so many died as before. As each family group lost less to the process of survival of the fittest, they moved north and south, but most of all, they moved south.

ANCIENT INHABITANTS OF NORTH AMERICAN CONTINENT

Through hundreds of years, this process took place until this new race had spread like a fan into the Great Slave Lake region of Canada and turned south into the central part of the United States. As they moved and increased, they prospered and learned.

They learned to make better clothes, to guard against the still cold winters, to build better shelters and to find better caves, in which to live. The women learned more about finding edible fruits and berries around the camping areas. Sometimes, the men banded together to surround a herd of bison and drive them over a cliff so they became very easy prey to spear and stone. When the first series of Asiatic men wandered out of Asia and on to the North American continent, a great part of what is now the Western States, was a vast plain that had once been an inland sea. Upon this plain grazed animals, that provided sufficient food for these wandering tribes. As time passed, and the numbers of men gradually increased, it became very difficult for all to find enough wild meat to satisfy their needs. Some turned to gathering fruits and berries and others turned to finding ways to trap fish and other aquatic life.

Down through the great plains of the west and into Old Mexico, gradually moved the forerunners of what we now call the Aztec and Mayan People.

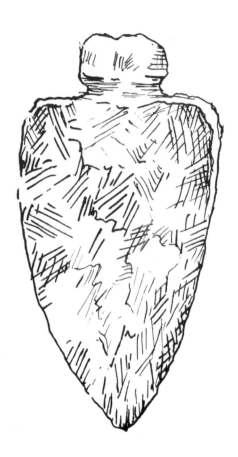

These tribes found an environment in which they no longer had to spend every waking hour in search of enough food to keep from starving. They had time to use their brains to begin to solve the mysteries of the earth and of mankind.

About five thousand years before the death of Christ, some of the forerunners of the Cherokees conceived the idea of tying animal sinew to a bent piece of wood to make the first bow and arrow. This invention was probably the greatest single step mankind had made since his discovery of the use of fire. With the bow and arrow, the hunter could easily kill game of all kind. He did not have to roam nearly as far afield as he had before. He could lie in wait for game and with this silent weapon, slay it before it was aware that he was near.

About this same time, some of the southeastern peoples discovered they could live on the fresh water mussels that existed abundantly in the broad Southern Rivers.

About fifteen hundred years after the invention of the bow and arrow, some intelligent ancient woman somewhere, picked up a ball of clay and fashioned it into a crude bowl that became the first clay vessel in existence. From that day on, the civilization of the American Indian rapidly moved forward. The women began to learn to cook in clay vessels and to decorate them in such a manner so that now, in modern times, anthropologists can tell what ancient tribe made which vessel. As these ancient women wandered with their men from one camp site to another, they picked berries and plants which were good to eat. They brought these plants and berries into their camps and ate them as part of their food. It was the habit of early nomadic people to move from one camp site to another so often they came back to the same camping sites year after year. Around these sites began to grow, from the refuse of previous visits, the seed from the berries that were gathered and eaten from former visits. Again, it was the women that realized the importance of having the plants grow near the camp sites. So they began to place the seeds in the ground on purpose. Thus began agriculture. Of course it was a long slow process of learning before these women found out that the ground should

be cleaned and broken and that the biggest and healthiest seed would produce the best plants. But this did happen, and especially important in the growth and selection process was the gradual evolution of corn from a seed bearing grass into a large plant that produced ears. With the development of corn as a food product that would feed a people from one season to another, a new security was found. For now, when the game ceased to be abundant, it was no longer necessary to pick up and move to another hunting area. The corn could be stored in dry vessels and used when the winters came.

When the problem of a constant food supply was overcome, the people naturally turned to solving other needs. One was the building of houses that would not rot and yet would keep out the miserable rain and cold in the winter. Another was the problem of protection from other tribes that might raid their villages and carry away what food supplies were on hand for the coming winter. This work and the fashioning of better and more durable tools took a great deal of the new leisure time.

Most of the permanent villages in the southeast were located on good-sized streams, usually where a smaller stream came into the larger one. The towns in the Cherokee Country ordinarily were built near the bank of the stream so that the occupants of the village were close to a source of fish and fresh water. The outer edge of the town was surrounded by a stockade that was built by placing good-sized posts in the ground about six inches apart. This space between the posts was woven with saplings and vines so that the stockade served as a protection against surprise attacks by enemies. Usually, there was an elaborate entrance-way that could be closed or effectively defended during an enemy attack. The houses of the villages began to be constructed of logs. These logs were placed vertically as closely together as possible in a kind of rough square that formed the outer walls of the house. These walls were reinforced by weaving vines and pliable pieces of wood between the upright posts. After they had been reinforced in this manner, a thick coat of mud was plastered over this framework to form an airtight wall. The roof of this type of house was constructed of saplings interwoven so that they formed a kind of dome over the four plastered walls. The dome was then covered with mats of long grasses and reeds. At first, all the cooking facilities were out in the open but later, fireplaces were built in the center of the structures with a fire hole to allow the smoke to escape.

Instead of going day by day to hunt for wild berries and plants, the women now went from the village houses to their garden plots, where they dug, planted, weeded and harvested. The daughters were taken along to learn how to plant and culti-

vate and harvest the maize and other vegetables. A daughter inherited her mother's garden plot or cleared her own. The men had little to do with the farming. It was their job to do the hunting. When the women first started planting crops, they probably used sharpened sticks to loosen up the soil but later, they began to use stone hoes and spades of very good quality. They even fashioned themselves brush arbors under which to sit in the heat of the day.

Although the first villages were little more than elaborate camp sites, the later ones were far more elaborate. They contained permanent houses and

stockades, meeting grounds and game grounds. And most of all, they afforded protection from weather and hostile tribes. Naturally, with this added protection and stable food production, the population of agricultural tribes increased by leaps and bounds. Where before there was a miserable little village huddled on the bank of a stream, now the village became a thriving, busy town with public meeting house and broad cleared fields surrounding the stockades. The men had learned to fashion a long log into a canoe so that it could be paddled up and down streams in quest of fish and game. No longer did the young warriors die in the prime of their ability. They lived to become wily, crafty leaders who directed and guided the efforts of the young. They lived to be old men, who sat in the public houses and told marvelous tales of their youth and tales of the world beyond the forests. They learned that they could charm and mystify the young by these tales and thus became men who were so powerful that no one dared question their judgment.

This development of tribes of people, who lived in houses and built villages was true in many parts of the United States but did not hold true where the land would not produce a suitable supply of staple food products. In other parts of the Middle West and Northwest, the tribes still wandered from one hunting ground to another in search for enough food on which to live. These tribes, although they advanced some in the complexity of their social structure, remained a great deal like the old nomadic hunters who first populated the North American Continent.

The Cherokees were among the Southeastern Indians, who had developed a complex way of living by the time the first white man touched the United States. They built houses, wove cloth, made vessels of clay and most important of all, organized into a loosely-knit tribal confederation.

The first and rather doubtful record of a reference to the Cherokees as a tribe of people, is found in one of the letters of DeSoto's men. This letter spoke of them as being a tribe that lived in the region that is now South Carolina. How the Cherokees came to the Eastern part of the United States is only a matter of conjecture but the best authorities believe they were a part of the Iroquoian people, who migrated from the west or northwest about thirty-five hundred years before the coming of the white man. During the period preceding the advent of the white man, the Cherokees were a part of a large group of people, who adjusted their ways of life to the eastern woodlands.

Naturally, the first travelers who came in contact with the tribes of Indians who lived along the eastern half of the United States did not make detailed studies of their cultures. They observed and recorded their outward acts but did not give a studied report on the whys and wherefores of these actions. Consequently, the only way we have of knowing their affairs, is by judging from the things they left and by the reports of later travelers who did really observe and record their findings.

TEACHING THE YOUNG

II   The Early Times

By the time the first white travelers on the American continent began to record some of their observations about Indians, the Cherokee people had developed a rather advanced culture that probably was exceeded only by civilized tribes of the Southwest; Mayan and Aztec groups. The social structure of the Cherokee people consisted of a form of clan kinship, in which there were seven recognized clans. All members of a clan were considered blood brothers and sisters, and were bound by honor to defend any member of that clan from wrong. Each clan, the Bird, Paint, Deer, Wolf, Blue, Long Hair, and Wild Potato were represented in the civil council by a counselor or counselors. The chief of the tribe was selected from one of these clans and did not inherit his office from his kinsmen. Actually, there were two chiefs, a Peace chief and a War chief. The Peace chief served when the tribe was at peace but the minute war was declared, the War chief was in command.

Most of the children's training was done by the women, at least until the boys became young men. The boy's training then was delegated to a relative, who taught the boy to track, to shoot the bow and arrow and defend himself against aggression. A young boy who aspired to becoming a recognized warrior had to be able to perform certain feats before he could win his feather. He also had to be able to prove himself in battle. Once a boy won his eagle feather, he wore it the rest of his life as a symbol that he was a warrior.

Sometimes, parents wished their children to become priests or medicine men. When they did, these children were turned over to older medicine men who did the entire upbringing of these chosen ones.

Such children were not allowed to associate with other children in the ordinary manner. They must always be about the business of becoming medicine men. They must stay in the company of those who trained them, at all times. They must go through endless hours of rigorous training that would try every part of their minds and bodies. They must ever attend the long talk sessions of the medicine men and always listen to tales of the distant past. They were taught the use of herbs and barks; also the rituals of cleansing and the art of purification. They must retain about themselves always an air of reserve and mystery. Their secrets were guarded with a silence that no outsider dared try penetrate. Their subsistence came in the form of payment for services rendered, but the power and honor of being a medicine man was the greatest tribute a man could be paid, for chiefs and great warriors might come and go but medicine men were medicine men of all times.

Probably the greatest single honor that could come to a woman would be to become a sacred one. Only by a great heroic deed did she become so. This deed had to be recognized as of major importance to the tribe and to its people. Once a woman was recognized as the sacred woman, she had many privileges. She sat in council as an equal to other counselors. She had the ear of important members of the tribe and she often had the say whether a prisoner or captive lived or died. It was probably just such a sacred woman whom DeSoto called a queen, and whom he captured for his guide, to lead him into the Cherokee Country. In fact, women had about as much to say about the business of the tribe as the men did. They were not considered slaves as they were in some of the more primitive tribes. They participated in almost all social events of the tribe and quite often were the main attraction in various types of ceremonies. The provision of food was in their hands, except the killing of wild game. They trained the children, made the crops and clothes, did the cooking and

NEW FIRE CEREMONY

helped build the houses. It was probably this acceptance of the importance of the women's position that helped make the Cherokee people a great deal farther advanced than that of their neighbors.

The passage of time revolved around the new fire festival, in which the old year ended and the new began. At this time, the fire places in all houses were cleaned of ashes and the fires put out completely. After a great and elaborate ceremony, in which the seven clans had a hand, the sacred fire in the council house was lighted to signify the beginning of the new year. The fires in the village

were then relighted from this sacred fire so that they might have the benefits of its magical properties.

As a part of the new fire ceremony, the village participated in an Indian ball game, which was called in their language, *the little war*. The game probably got this name from the fact that it was as rough as any game could be without going to war. In the game, the players could do almost anything to get the ball away from an opposing player. The object of the game was to take a walnut-sized ball from the center of a large field between two goal posts that were placed at equal distance from the center ground. The game was played always by an equal number of players on each side. Those playing could number from ten to sixty to a side and each player was matched against an individual from the opposing team.

The game was started when an old man tossed the ball up at the center ground for the two team leaders to try to knock the ball toward their own goal post. The ball sticks used by the teams were about two feet long and cupped at one end so that the ball could be picked up from the ground without touching it with the hands. Once the ball was tossed up and struck by one of the captains of the teams, the mad scramble for it was on. Pushing and shoving, tripping and knocking each other, all the players attempted to pick the ball up off the ground. Once the ball was picked up, the player getting the ball usually placed it in his mouth so that he might have both hands to defend himself.

Broken arms and legs, kicked in teeth and cracked heads were not uncommon because anything went. The only thing not allowed was to pick the ball off the ground with the hands.

The first team to get twenty points was the winner and collector of all the bets that were made before the game started.

The planting of corn, the first roasting ear time and the full ripe time of the corn ear were all celebrated by elaborate ceremonies that sometimes stretched over many days. The preparation for the ceremonies were as elaborate and mystical as the actual ceremony itself.

According to the Cherokee myth keepers, at one time all things living were in the sky, on the sky rock and this was before the world was made. And at one time all living things spoke the same language, so they understood each other and could understand all things that were done, but man misused this privilege and was stricken deaf to the talk of the animals and birds. The Great One, who was over the sky rock, punished man so that he could only understand the talk of his own kind. As the animals, birds and insects grew in population, the sky rock became crowded with the over population, until there was danger of some being pushed off. So a council was called of all the animals to decide what was to be done about the situation. Up to this time, the earth had been floating around the sky rock, covered with a sea of water that extended from end to end. The animals thought it would be of no use to them because there was no way they could live on a world that was covered with water.

Finally, the water beetle was sent down to see if he could find a single place on this sea of water where the animals could go to live. When he finally succeeded in getting down on the ocean of water, he swam around until he could see that there was no place for the animals to go so he dived down under the water and found mud, which he brought to the surface. This mud began to grow and grow until, after a long time, it covered much of the world's surface but it was still too wet for anyone to live on. When the water beetle returned to the sky rock and made his report, the animals were very sorry and afraid that some must now be pushed off the sky rock and perish. The grandfather buzzard, the father of all buzzards, said that he would go down to the world and see if he could find a place. He said the water beetle was very small and could not cover great distances as he could, so he would be able to cover a greater part of the world than the little water beetle. So, down to the world he went and began to fly over its surface, until he had spent a long time flying over muddy parts of the world and over the great ocean. Finally he grew so weary from his constant searching that his giant wing tips began to dip down into the muddy surface of the world. This wing dipping made great holes in the mud and mighty mountains where his breast was. These great holes became valleys and the ridges became great mountains and that was how the Great Smoky Mountains came to be. They were the first mountains and they began to dry out so it was not too long a time until they were dry enough for the animals and birds and bees and all other things to come down from the rock.

III   The Colonial Period

Once white men had seen the vast untamed wilderness of America, the fate of the Indian was sealed. The white men first came in small parties with pretensions of friendliness to the Indians. Then they came in larger parties with more gear and less friendliness. Then they came with their plows and fences and their greedy need for land. Some remained friendly but others took what lay in their paths and called it theirs, because it belonged to a people whom they considered savage. And to them, a savage had no rights nor consideration. As each new shipload emptied its spawn of human cargo from the hovels and fetters of the old world, they spread and grew and moved into the new land. At first, they were mostly met with curiosity and awe, but then, after more and more came to build cabins and fences, upon what had once been fertile forests and untamed wilderness, the Indians began to resist and to wonder where it would all end. The Indians themselves had no real need for land as individuals, because they did no great amount of farming, but the forests and rivers they did need, for when the trees were cut and the rivers occupied with towns and villages, there no longer remained any game upon which the Indians could live. The Indians asked the officials of the colonies to hold back the ever-swelling tide to certain boundaries, and when this failed, they began to try to stem the tide, as they had in other times with their own kind. Indian warfare was not of a kind the colonist had ever known before. It was a savage and a ruthless war that left women and children in villages and towns without protection or mercy.

For nearly a hundred years after the visit of DeSoto, the Cherokees had very little contact with white men. A small party of Spaniards is known to have traveled through the Cherokee Country, much as DeSoto did, but these early comers established no permanent settlements. Later, the Spaniards did try to set up mining operations within the outskirts of the Cherokee Country, but these did not remain as permanent fixtures. The secret policy maintained by the Spanish Government left no records of the success of their mining operations.

The first known contact the British Settlements had with the Cherokee occurred at Richmond, Virginia. The English had been at war with the Powhatin Tribe at the James River Falls, for a considerable time. They had no sooner driven out the Powhatins than the village site was reoccupied by a large force of Cherokee. It had taken a considerable effort to dislodge the Powhatins from the site and to have it reoccupied immediately by another was almost too much for the English. They became very alarmed and called in over a hundred Pamunky warriors to help them destroy the new intruders.

The combined forces marched against the Cherokee, but received such a beating they were forced to sue for peace.

The first known English settlement of South Carolina occurred in 1670 and the first known treaty signed by a Cherokee chief occurred in 1684. By the early seventeen hundreds, regular skirmishes were occurring between the races. The Governor of South Carolina was accused of commissioning agents to take Indians as slaves during a time that the Cherokee and the English colonies were at peace. Quite often the Cherokee joined the English in war against tribes with whom they themselves were unfriendly. They did this with the Tuscarora and with the help of the English forced them out of the Carolinas by 1713. Two years later, they refused to join the Yamassee conspiracy that resulted in a great massacre of the whites by the Yamassee and as a result of this refusal, the Creeks burned and sacked the Cherokee villages. Thus began the destruction that would last over a hundred years and in the end would completely destroy all the Cherokee towns.

Between the years seventeen hundred and seventeen hundred sixty-three, the different tribes that lay between the Spanish, French and English colonies were political pawns for the different interests of these various nations. One great difference existed between the way the English treated the Indians and the way the Spanish and French treated them. The French, particularly, mingled and mixed with them freely. Their traders often married Indian women and settled down within the tribes to continue to serve their mother country as well as being a part of the Indian tribal life. The English did this very seldom. They looked down on the Indians' way of life and associated with them only when forced to. This was particularly so after a few generations of the English had grown up along the frontier. The frontiersmen feared and hated the Indians and lost few opportunities to do them harm. By 1773, three different treaties had taken from the Cherokee all the great hunting territory that lay between the Cumberland and Kentucky Rivers. Constant pressure of the ever-moving and expanding English settlements along the Holston and Tennessee Rivers gradually moved the Indian towns and settlements before them. One treaty would hardly be signed before another would be in order because the white settlers would have moved into new Indian territory before the old treaty could be ratified. By the time the American Revolution broke out in 1776, the Indians were firmly aligned against the Frontier Americans. To the Indians, the British Government stood as the only symbol of authority. They were well aware that they could expect very little quarter from the frontier government.

By the latter part of 1776, the Indians and Tories began attacking the frontier settlements all along the coast of South Carolina and Georgia.

Isolated homes and farmsteads felt the tomahawk and scalping knife. Charleston, South Carolina came under attack from British men of war and Torie and Indian forces attacking it.

The Holston settlements in Tennessee were the objects of seven hundred marching Cherokee warriors and would have undoubtedly been completely destroyed if it hadn't been for the heroic warning of Nancy Ward, a friendly Indian woman. As it was, the Tennesseans were able to defeat the Cherokee in a bloody battle at a place called Long Island.

Realizing the danger of constant harassment from the Indians and the necessity of being on the alert for the British, the American leaders in South Carolina, North Carolina, Virginia, and Georgia decided that expeditionary forces from four sides into the Indian Country would forestall much of the danger that would result from attempting to defend all the eastern frontiers. As a result, an Army 2,400 strong, under General Griffith Rutherford, crossed the Blue Ridge Mountains and struck at the very heart of the Cherokee homeland. Towns that had never before felt the vengeance of the white soldiers were completely destroyed. All the Indian towns along the Oconaluftee and Tuckaseegee Rivers felt the impact of the torch and musket. There occurred a pitched battle near Wayah Bald between Rutherford's forces and the Cherokee, high in the Nantahala Mountains.

In late September, the South Carolina forces under the command of Col. Andrew Williamson intercepted Rutherford's forces at Murphy, North Carolina. This juncture served to complete the raids on the Cherokee towns in Georgia and North Carolina. Meanwhile, the Virginia forces under Col. William Christian marched down the great Indian war trail to the Long Island on the Holston. Here they gathered additional North Carolina forces and what men were available from the Tennessee garrisons. This combined force made their way against Indian and Tory forces drawn up to oppose them at a crossing on the French Broad River. However, when the Indians saw what a formidable force they were facing, they withdrew without resistance, thus allowing the Revolutionary army to continue through the Indian towns on the Little Tennessee River. By the time the army arrived at the Indian towns on the Little Tennessee, the people had fled, leaving all they owned for the Army to destroy and burn. This destruction made most of the remaining Cherokee Tribe realize the futility of further resistance. So they sent the important men of the tribe to sue for peace. This was done and peace finally established.

By the treaties that were negotiated after the intrusion of the North Carolina, Georgia, and Virgina armies, the Cherokees lost all their lands in South Carolina, everything in Tennessee to the Blue Ridge Mountains and had to suffer under the eyes of an agent who watched their actions for signs of hostility towards the new states. Many of the die-hard Cherokee moved out of their original home territory and settled far down the Tennessee River, to become a thorn in the sides of the colonists until their towns were destroyed again about three years later. This group remained a hostile group for as long as they existed as a group of people. They were under the implacable leadership of the great Dragging Canoe who would not concede to those who had destroyed his way of life.

British forces, with the active assistance of their Indian allies, had by the early part of 1780 taken all of Georgia and South Carolina. Their armies were preparing to move northward into North Carolina and Virginia when they made the mistake of demanding the surrender of the mountain men who up to this time had spent their efforts in fighting off the Indian allies of the British. The mountain men assembled, and under leadership of their own choosing, began the march of King's Mountain, South Carolina, that spelled the defeat of the British in the South.

Thus the burning of the Indian towns and the defeat of the British at King's Mountain left the Cherokee at the mercy of the frontier Americans.

INDIAN ALPHABET

D	R	T	Ꮼ	O	i
a	e	i	o	u	v

ga	ka	ge	gi	go	gu	gv

ha	he	hi	ho	hu	hv

la	le	li	lo	lu	lv

ma	me	mi	mo	mu	

nu	hna	gna	ne	ni	no	nu	nv

qna	qne	qni	qno	qnu	qnv

sa	s	se	si	sa	su	sv

da	ta	de	te	di	ti	do	du	dv

dla	tla	tlo	tli	tlo	tlu	tlv

tsa	tse	tsi	tso	tsu	tsv

wa	we	wi	wo	wu	wv

ya	ye	yi	yo	yu	yv

A as in FATHER

E as A in HATE
OR SHORT as IN PIT

I as I in PIQUE
OR SHORT as IN PIT

O as in LOW
SHORT as IN NOT

U as OO in FOOT
SHORT as IN PULL

V SHORT U NAZALIZED

THERE WAS NO
SOUND OF
P, B, J, R, CH OR Z

The entire
language
could be
spoken
without
closing
the lips
except
for the
sound of "M"

IV   Sequoyah

GEORGE GUESS OR GEORGE GIST

Sequoyah was probably the greatest of all Cherokees. He is the only man in the history of mankind to invent a complete alphabet, without being able to read or write any other language. Not only was Sequoyah a great man of letters, but he was instrumental in always advising the Cherokees in a path of wisdom and tolerance.

He was born near Fort Loudoun, Tennessee in the village of Tuskegee. His mother was a full-blood Cherokee and his father probably was Nathaniel Gist, the famous scout and soldier. Nathaniel Gist's family supposedly recognized Sequoyah as Gist's son. When Sequoyah was a small boy, his mother removed to Alabama to an Indian settlement near Willstown. Here, Sequoyah spent most of his early life, learning to trace honey bees, to shoot the bow and arrow and to look after his mother's small farm.

The exact date of Sequoyah's birth is not known but army records show that he was old enough to fight in the Creek war of 1812 in company with a group of Cherokee volunteers. He, along with Junaluska, another famous Cherokee, fought with Andrew Jackson in the battle of Horseshoe Bend. It was only four years after this famous battle that he signed one of the many treaties in which the Government took a great part of the Cherokee lands.

There are many stories about when and how Sequoyah started working and thinking about his alphabet. One of these stories is that he and some of his friends fell into a discussion about writing, after having heard the Bible translated at a white man's house.

SEQUOYAH OR GEORGE GIST

as he appeared in 1828 to Charles Bird King, who did his portrait in Washington, D.C. He wears the medal given him by the Cherokee Nation as a token of appreciation for the invention of the Cherokee alphabet.

His friends said that writing was a most wonderful thing, to be able to put all the wisdom down on the talking leaves so that they would not be forgotten. Sequoyah, hearing this remark, said, "I could do this thing that the white man does." His friends laughed and said, "You are foolish, you could not even begin to do this wonderful thing. This has taken many long winters for the white man to do. It is his gift. The Great One has not given us this gift. It would be foolish for us even to try such a task." But Sequoyah did not hear their last remark. He was already turning over in his mind how he was going to put his own talk down on the talking leaves.

Through the hours and the days and the years he worked. He worked against the ridicule of his friends, the threats of his enemies and the active opposition of his wife. Once, she even burned every scrap of bark and material he had scribbled on, in an effort to stop him from his task. But it was of no use because he knew that eventually he would find a way to write his own language. His friends tried to dissuade him from his task; his enemies told dark tales about the evils he would bring down on his people by delving into the gifts of the white men. When they passed his house, they gave his home hostile stares and did not speak to Sequoyah nor his family.

Sequoyah began his efforts by trying to devise a symbol for every Cherokee word. When he had devised several thousand symbols, he began to see that this was useless because it would be impossible to remember so many marks. Then he tried to figure out a way to make a symbol for a sentence. But this too, he saw would not do because there were so many ways to make a sentence. Eventually, he began to listen for the different sounds that the Cherokee language had. These, he would record with a mark that he thought would be easy to remember. Soon, he ran out of ideas for new marks; his signs began to all look alike. For a long time he did not know what to do. Then, while walking one day, he found a piece of old newspaper that he discovered was full of symbols, which he had never even thought of making. Thus, Sequoyah not knowing one English letter from another, used a great many of our own crooked marks to represent sounds in the Cherokee language.

Listening to his children, the few friends who would still come about him and to complete strangers, Sequoyah eventually worked out the eighty-six symbols that represented all the sounds in his language, thus bringing to the Cherokee people a way of writing their language so that now, they could have their own newspapers, books and Bibles. It was a great day that would bring everlasting fame to Sequoyah.

While Sequoyah was thinking and working on his alphabet, the tides of his own life were ever shifting and moving. The treaty of 1816 had stipulated that any Cherokees who wanted to remove to the Indian territory in Arkansas, could do so.

One of Sequoyah's friends, Chief John Jolly, took his family and a small group of friends and moved out to the Cherokee country of the Skin Bayou section of Arkansas. Sequoyah accompanied this group.

Two years later, Jolly returned to the Cherokee settlements of Alabama and persuaded a second group to emigrate to the Arkansas territory. Sequoyah, who made the second trip with the Chief, had completed his alphabet and was able to take letters from the Western Cherokees to the Eastern Cherokees in Alabama. There was a great deal of interest in his mode of putting down the language. Some of Sequoyah's friends became interested in learning to read and write Sequoyah's alphabet. He taught these people and they in turn taught others. Some of the quicker ones learned to read and write in three or four days. It was not long until nearly all the Cherokee people were interested in learning to read and write their language. The council, in 1824, recognized the greatness of Sequoyah's alphabet by voting him a medal of honor and a letter of recognition. In 1825, an educated Cherokee by the name of David Brown began the translation of the Bible in Cherokee, and by 1828 Dr. Samuel Worcester, a missionary to the Eastern Cherokees, had been successful in having a printing press made in Boston. The printing press was shipped to Charleston, S. C. and up the river to Augusta, Ga. It was taken by wagon two hundred miles inland to New Echota, Georgia. New Echota at that time was the Eastern Capital of the Cherokee Nation. Elias Boudinot, another educated Cherokee, was made the editor-in-chief of the new paper, *The Phoenix*. This paper printed news in both English and Cherokee.

These times were not easy for the Cherokee people. Sequoyah was sent as a member of a delegation from the Arkansas group, to appeal to the Federal Government in Washington for help in defending the lands and people from encroaching whites. This group did not go to make the Treaty

MOLLY RUNNINGWOLF SEQUOYAH

MOLLY RUNINGWOLF
SEGUOYAH.

J. ANCHUTIN
1957.

of 1828, that was a result of their visit to Washington, but went to try to straighten out various land claims from the Government and to appeal the grievances against the encroaching whites. However, the Treaty that was worked out as a result of their visit was really good for the Western Cherokees. Sequoyah's visit in the nation's Capital did not go unnoted. His fame was already established from the invention of the alphabet and many people were interested in seeing the man of such unusual gift. His picture was painted by Charles Bird King, and he was the subject of lectures by Samuel Lorenzo Knapp. In describing Sequoyah, his admirers noted that he did not discard his native costume nor his innate dignity.

Turbulent times for the Cherokees were ahead; great pressures were being put on the Eastern Cherokees to remove to Oklahoma. Some did voluntarily remove but the main body of the people wanted to stay in their home country of Tennessee, North Carolina and Georgia. They besieged the Government with requests for the Treaty of 1828 to be set aside. They claimed it was not legal, in that the true Chief of the Cherokees did not approve nor sign it. But this was of no avail. The order for removal was given by President Andrew Jackson and the fatal day set.

The arrival of the Eastern Cherokee in the Oklahoma territory was of much concern to the old settlers as they called themselves. Their government was already established and the people of influence felt the new arrivals should answer only to the will of the people who were already there. This attitude caused much ill feeling, because the newcomers far outnumbered the old settlers.

The final settlement of the differences between these two factions was partly brought about by the wisdom of Sequoyah and his recognition of the rights of others. When the council meetings were held, that eventually led to the forming of a workable Tribal Government, it was Sequoyah's wise counseling that led to the peaceful solution of a conflict that had already taken the lives of three important Cherokees.

By the time the Cherokees had established their government and had begun to prosper in their new homes, Sequoyah's mind turned to wonder about the Cherokees in Mexico and Texas, who had suffered much at the hands of raiders. In earlier years, when these people had been attacked and nearly wiped out in Texas, he extended to them an invitation to come to the Arkansas Cherokee country to live. Many did so, but not all. It was this remnant that Sequoyah was interested in seeing. Although, by this time Sequoyah had grown old and unwell, he was determined to go to Mexico to find and see these lost Cherokees. He gathered a party of eight of his close and trusted friends to travel the unknown trails into a hostile country. In this summer of 1842, Sequoyah left his home in Oklahoma, never to return.

The story of his journey is one of hunger, lost horses, floods, sickness and in the end, death in an unknown grave on foreign soil. The trail of Sequoyah's life leads many places, from the hill country of Tennessee to the low country of Alabama, from the low country to the wanderings of a soldier, from the wanderings of a soldier to the life of a father, the life of a father to Bayou country of Arkansas, from Arkansas to Oklahoma, from Oklahoma to the Nation's Capital. From the Nation's Capital to the Cherokee Capital and from there to the climactic pilgrimage to the lost Cherokee in Mexico. Although there are no stone slabs over his grave to mark Sequoyah's passing, the honor to his name and to his people will ever remain in the timeless Sequoyah redwood trees that were named for him and the alphabet that he alone invented.

REMOVAL OF CHEROKEES TO WESTERN RESERVATION

V The Cherokee Removal

In a mountain cove, close by the Oconaluftee River, stood a small group of log cabins, where the blue smoke rose in the early morning of August, 1838. A Cherokee Indian child played with a stone marble in one of the yards, while his mother cooked fatback on the hearth fireplace inside. Unseen by the two, a small detachment of soldiers carefully began the encirclement of the cabins. At a signal from the sergeant in charge, six armed men appeared at the front doors. The mother, hearing the noisy soldiers, rushed to the front door and started to grab the child. She was too late.

Thus began the final chapter of the Eastern Cherokee Nation. The beginning of the end of a proud people was at hand. With bowed heads and all they owned on their backs, those who had stubbornly remained in their eastern homeland were being forced into stockades and gathering places so that they could start on the nine hundred mile exodus across the Mississippi into Oklahoma. No day in all America's history is blacker nor no deed more shameful than the forced removal of a peaceful tribe of people who asked only to be let alone in peace and understanding.

In less than a hundred years, the Cherokees had lost all of a vast domain that included parts of West Virginia, Virginia, Kentucky, Tennessee, North Carolina, South Carolina, Georgia, and Alabama. Treaty after treaty had squeezed the boundaries of their holdings ever inward until at last there remained no more.

In 1721, the first treaty was made with the Cherokees by Governor Nicholson. Just a little over a hundred years later, in 1835, the Cherokees lost all of what little land remained to them. This hundred years had been a time of constant pressure on the Indian land with treaties sometimes forced upon them at the rate of two a year. Other lands not obtained by treaties were simply occupied and held by frontier families.

The state of Georgia was particularly abusive toward the Cherokees. And in the final years of their existence as a tribe of people in the East, Georgia systematically refused to recognize the decisions of the Court and the law of the land in regard to them.

Some authorities are of the opinion that the discovery of gold near Dahlonega, Georgia was the crowning event that led the Georgia authorities and the people of that state to believe that vast riches lay hidden in the wilds of the Cherokee Country. Undoubtedly this event had some influence on the Georgians and others, but probably the ill feeling existing between the frontiersmen and the Indians was the greatest contributing factor in the move to rid the East of the Cherokees.

In the Revolutionary War, the Cherokees had been allies of the British against the frontier Americans. The constant need for new land for the ever expanding population of the Americans, naturally led to a distrust and hatred between those who were taking the land and those losing it. It was this need for land and the hate of those who held it that led to the final disposition of the Cherokee Nation.

Andrew Jackson, himself a frontiersman, aided the forces in Georgia that finally pushed the Indians off their lands. When Georgia annexed the Cherokee lands and the Supreme Court of the United States ruled against them, it was Jackson who said, "The Court has made its decision now let them enforce it."

It was also Jackson's life that had been saved by a great Cherokee by the name of Junaluska at the Battle of Horse Shoe Bend.

Although many people spoke up for the rights of the Tribe in the United States Congress and in editorial comment, their forces were not strong enough to force the cancellation of the treaty which stipulated they were to be removed by May 26, 1838.

The cause of the Cherokee was championed by the great Henry Clay, Daniel Webster, and Davy Crockett, but even those three notable statesmen failed and on May 10, 1838 General Winfield Scott issued the general order for forced removal. The Cherokee were to be rounded up and placed in stockades at designated points so that at a given time all could be brought together and started west.

Many of the Cherokees died in the stockades as a result of heartbreak and malnutrition. Although the army provided what it considered a sufficient ration for each person, they failed to consider that the diet of most of the people was entirely different from the kind provided for at the hastily prepared assembly points. The Cherokees as a result became weakened and subject to all the ailments to which they were exposed.

The mountains, hills and flat country of Georgia and North Carolina were filled with soldiers until all but a handful of the Cherokees were herded into the stockades and ready for removal. The few mountain Cherokees that hid out in the deepest forests and most inaccessible places escaped the dragnet set for them. Those who escaped are the forefathers of the Eastern Cherokee who now live on the Qualla Indian Reservation.

In the following account, Pvt. John Burnett of the United States Cavalry tells the story of the actual removal more graphically and sympathetically than all the history book accounts in existence.

THE TRAIL OF TEARS

JOHN BURNETT'S JOURNEY

Birthday Story of Private John G. Burnett, Captain Abraham McClellan's Company, 2nd Regiment, 2nd Brigade, Mounted Infantry, Cherokee Indian Removal 1838-39.

This is my birthday December the 11th 1890, I am eighty years old today. I was born at Kings Iron Works in Sullivan County, Tennessee, December the 11th, 1810. I grew into manhood fishing in Beaver Creek and roaming through the forest hunting the Deer the wild Boar and the timber Wolf. Often spending weeks at a time in the solitary wilderness with no companions but my rifle, hunting knife, and a small hatchet that I carried in my belt in all of my wilderness wanderings.

On these long hunting trips I met and became acquainted with many of the Cherokee Indians, hunting with them by day and sleeping around their camp fires by night. I learned to speak their language, and they taught me the arts of trailing and building traps and snares. On one of my long hunts in the fall of 1829 I found a young Cherokee who had been shot by a roving band of hunters and who had eluded his pursuers and concealed himself under a shelving rock. Weak from loss of blood the poor creature was unable to walk and almost famished for water. I carried him to a spring bathed and bandaged the bullet wound, built a shelter out of bark peeled from a dead chestnut tree, nursed and protected him feeding him on chestnuts and roasted deer meat. When he was able to travel I accompanied him to the home of his people and remained so long that I was given up for lost. By this time I had become an expert rifleman and fairly good archer and a good trapper and spent most of my time in the forest in quest of game.

The removal of the Cherokee Indians from their life long homes in the year of 1838 found me a young man in the prime of life and a Private soldier in the American Army. Being acquainted with many of the Indians and able to fluently speak their language, I was sent as interpreter into the Smoky Mountain Country in May, 1838, and witnessed the execution of the most brutal order in the History of American Warfare. I saw the helpless Cherokees arrested and dragged from their homes, and driven at the bayonet point into the stockades. And in the chill of a drizzling rain on an October morning I saw them loaded like cattle or sheep into six hundred and forty-five wagons and started toward the west.

One can never forget the sadness and solemnity of that morning. Chief John Ross led in prayer and when the bugle sounded and the wagons started rolling many of the children rose to their feet and waved their little hands good-by to their mountain homes, knowing they were leaving them forever. Many of these helpless people did not have blankets and many of them had been driven from home barefooted.

On the morning of November the 17th we encountered a terrific sleet and snow storm with freezing temperatures and from that day until we reached the end of the fateful journey on March the 26th 1839, the sufferings of the Cherokees were awful. The trail of the exiles was a trail of death. They had to sleep in the wagons and on the ground without fire. And I have known as many as twenty-two of them to die in one night of pneumonia due to ill treatment, cold, and exposure. Among this number was the beautiful Christian wife of Chief John Ross. This noble hearted woman died a martyr to childhood, giving her only blanket for the protection of a sick child. She rode thinly clad through a blinding sleet and snow storm, developed pneumonia and died in the still hours of a bleak winter night, with her head resting on Lieutenant Gregg's saddle blanket.

I made the long journey to the west with the Cherokees and did all that a Private soldier could do to alleviate their sufferings. When on guard duty at night I have many times walked my beat in my blouse in order that some sick child might have the warmth of my overcoat.

I was on guard duty the night Mrs. Ross died. When relieved at midnight I did not retire, but remained around the wagon out of sympathy for Chief Ross, and at daylight was detailed by Captain McClellan to assist in the burial like the other unfortunates who died on the way. Her uncoffined body was buried in a shallow grave by the roadside far from her native mountain home, and the sorrowing Cavalcade moved on.

Being a young man I mingled freely with the young women and girls. I have spent many pleasant hours with them when I was supposed to be under my blanket, and they have many times sung their mountain songs for me, this being all that they could do to repay my kindness. And with all my association with Indian girls from October 1829 to March 26th 1839, I did not meet one who was a moral prostitute. They are kind and tender hearted and many of them are beautiful.

The only trouble that I had with anybody on the entire journey to the west was a brutal teamster by the name of Ben McDonal, who was using his whip on an old feeble Cherokee to hasten him into the wagon. The sight of that old and nearly blind creature quivering under the lashes of a bull whip was too much for me. I attempted to stop McDonal and it ended in a personal encounter. He lashed me across the face, the wire tip on his whip cutting a bad gash in my cheek. The little hatchet that I had carried in my hunting days was in my belt, and McDonal was carried unconscious from the scene.

I was placed under guard but, Ensign Henry Bullock and Private Elkanah Millard had both witnessed the encounter. They gave Captain McClellan the facts and I was never brought to trial. Years later I met 2nd Lieutenant Riley and Ensign Bullock at Bristol at John Robersons show, and Bullock jokingly reminded me that there was a case still pending against me before a court martial and wanted to know how much longer I was going to have the trial put off?

McDonal finally recovered, and in the year 1851, was running on a boat out of Memphis, Tennessee.

The long painful journey to the west ended March 26th, 1839, with four-thousand silent graves reaching from the foothills of the Smoky Mountains to what is known as Indian territory in the West. And covetousness on the part of the white race was the cause of all that the Cherokees had to suffer.

Ever since Ferdinand DeSoto, made his journey through the Indian country in the year of 1540, there had been a tradition of a rich Gold mine somewhere in the Smoky Mountain Country, and I think the tradition was true. At a festival at Echata on Christmas night 1829, I danced and played with Indian girls who were wearing ornaments around their necks that looked Gold.

In the year of 1828, a little Indian boy living on Ward creek had sold a Gold nugget to a white trader, and that nugget sealed the doom of the Cherokees. In a short time the country was over run with armed brigands claiming to be Government Agents, who paid no attention to the rights of the Indians who were the legal possessors of the country. Crimes were committed that were a disgrace to civilization. Men were shot in cold blood, lands were confiscated. Homes were burned and the inhabitants driven out by these Gold hungry brigands.

Chief Junaluska was personally acquainted with President Andrew Jackson. Junaluska had taken five hundred of the flower of his Cherokee scouts and helped Jackson to win the battle of the Horse

Shoe leaving thirty-three of them dead on the field. And in that battle Junaluska had drove his Tomahawk through the skull of a Creek warrior, when the Creek had Jackson at mercy.

Chief John Ross sent Junaluska as an envoy to plead with President Jackson for protection for his people, but Jackson's manner was cold and indifferent toward the rugged son of the forest who had saved his life. He met Junaluska, heard his plea but curtly said "Sir your audience is ended, there is nothing I can do for you." The doom of the Cherokee was sealed, Washington D. C. had decreed that they must be driven West, and their lands given to the white man, and in May 1838 an Army of four thousand regulars, and three thousand volunteer soldiers under command of General Winfield Scott, marched into the Indian country and wrote the blackest chapter on the pages of American History.

Men working in the fields were arrested and driven to the stockades. Women were dragged from their homes by soldiers whose language they could not understand. Children were often separated from their parents and driven into the stockades with the sky for a blanket and the earth for a pillow. And often the old and infirm were prodded with bayonets to hasten them to the stockades.

In one home death had come during the night, a little sad faced child had died and was lying on a bear skin couch and some women were preparing the little body for burial. All were arrested and driven out leaving the child in the cabin. I don't know who buried the body.

In another home was a frail Mother, apparently a widow and three small children, one just a baby. When told that she must go the Mother gathered the children at her feet, prayed an humble prayer in her native tongue, patted the old family dog on the head, told the faithful creature good-by, with a baby strapped on her back and leading a child with each hand started on her exile. But the task was too great for that frail Mother. A stroke of heart failure relieved her sufferings. She sunk and died with her baby on her back, and her other two children clinging to her hands.

Chief Junaluska who had saved President Jackson's life at the battle of Horse Shoe witnessed this scene, the tears gushing down his cheeks and lifting his cap he turned his face toward the Heavens and said "Oh my God if I had known at the battle of the Horse Shoe what I know now American History would have been differently written."

At this time 1890 we are too near the removal of the Cherokees for our young people to fully understand the enormity of the crime that was committed against a helpless race, truth is. the facts are being concealed from the young people of today. School children of today do not know that we are living on lands that were taken from a helpless race at the bayonet point to satisfy the white man's greed for gold.

Future generations will read and condemn the act and I do hope posterity will remember the private soldiers like myself, and like the four Cherokees who were forced by General Scott, to shoot an Indian Chief and his children had to execute the orders of our superiors. We had no choice in the matter.

Twenty-five years after the removal it was my privilege to meet a large company of the Cherokees in uniform of the Confederate Army under Command of Colonel Thomas, they were encamped at Zollicoffer. I went to see them. Most of them were just boys at the time of the removal but they instantly recognized me as "the soldier that was good to us." Being able to talk to them in their native language I had an enjoyable day with them. From them I learned that Chief John Ross was still ruler of the nation in 1863. And I wonder if he is still living? He was a noble hearted fellow and suffered a lot for his race.

At one time he was arrested and thrown into a

dirty jail in an effort to break his spirit, but he remained true to his people and led them in prayer when they started on their exile. And his Christian wife sacrificed her life for a little girl who had pneumonia. The Anglo Saxon race should build a towering monument to perpetuate her noble act in giving her only blanket for comfort of a sick child. Incidentally the child recovered, but Mrs. Ross is sleeping in an unmarked grave far from her native Smoky Mountain home.

When Scott invaded the Indian country some of the Cherokees fled to caves and dens in the mountains and were never captured and they are there today. I have long intended going there and trying to find them but I have put off going from year to year and now I am too feeble to ride that far. The fleeting years have come and gone and old age has overtaken me, I can truthfully say that neither my rifle, nor my knife are stained with Cherokee blood.

I can truthfully say that I did my best for them when they certainly did need a friend. Twenty-five years after the removal I still lived in their Memory as "the soldier who was good to us."

However murder is murder whether committed by the villain skulking in the dark or by uniformed men stepping to the strains of martial music.

Murder is murder and somebody must answer, somebody must explain the streams of blood that flowed in the Indian country in the summer of 1838. Somebody must explain the four-thousand silent graves that mark the trail of the Cherokees to their exile. I wish I could forget it all, but the picture of six-hundred and forty-five wagons lumbering over the frozen ground with their Cargo of suffering humanity still lingers in my memory.

Let the Historian of a future day tell the sad story with its sighs, its tears and dying groans. Let the great Judge of all the earth weigh our actions and reward us according to our work.

Children—Thus ends my promised birthday story. This December the 11th 1890.

CHEROKEE RESERVATION TODAY

VI The Cherokee Today

The present-day Cherokee people are the descendants of those who hid out in the North Carolina mountains and of some few, who were allowed to stay by the army, during the removal in 1838. For a long time after the removal, the remnant of the once powerful tribe struggled desperately to exist. They could not legally hold land, and actually for a long time were not considered citizens. Their land, such as it was, was held through white friends or was left alone because no one thought it worth having. But gradually, this remnant people began to amass holdings in the Lufty River district. They were aided in this by a white Indian Trader named Colonel William Thomas, who would buy the land for individual Indians and hold it in his own name. He allowed the Cherokees to live on it and develop it until the time that he became a United States Senator and was able to get laws passed that recognized these people as citizens. Colonel Thomas had amassed a lot of lands for the Cherokees by the time that the law, allowing them to become citizens, was passed, but he had also amassed a considerable number of debts, so that when he died, the title to the Cherokee lands had not been legally settled. Upon Thomas' death, his creditors attempted to seize the Cherokee holdings that were still in Thomas' name. A delegation of the Cherokees was sent to Washington to appeal to the Federal Government, to keep the lands from being sold for Thomas' debts. This delegation was able to get the Government to appropriate twenty-five thousand dollars to clear the title to Cherokee holdings. This twenty-five thousand dollars was appropriated out of money that had not been paid to the Eastern Cherokees for removal to the West. Lawyers were hired and put to work clearing the titles to the lands. When these titles were cleared and some new tracts added to them through additional appropriations to the twenty-five thousand, this boundary became what is now known as the Cherokee Indian Reservation or the Qualla Boundary.

The Cherokees paid taxes on this land and developed it as any other citizen who lived in the state of North Carolina. The only difference in this land and other lands outside the reservation was, that the Cherokees could not sell any part of it without the permission of the Cherokee Council and the President of the United States. The status of the land, as far as selling it, remains the same today. The Cherokees cannot sell their land except to other recognized Cherokees.

After Thomas' death, the affairs of the Cherokees for awhile had no official guide nor councilor. Although the Government had ordered two official rolls of the people and had requested the Commissioner of Indian Affairs to take over the Administration of the Cherokee affairs, there had been nothing done up through the late 1870's. The Quakers, being long time friends of the Indians, realized that they needed schools and religious instruction. They established these facilities in Cherokee in 1881. The school was a contract school, partly supported by the Friends Society and partly by the Government. From all accounts, the Quakers were able to make a great deal of progress in forwarding the general education and welfare of the Cherokees. They worked sincerely and industriously towards their goal and the general effects are to be recognized today. After a ten-year period of the Quaker contract schools, the Federal Government was ready to carry on the School work and the administration of the Indian affairs.

The present-day Indian Reservation or Qualla Indian Boundary has approximately fifty-five thousand acres of lands in its boundaries and lies in the heart of Western North Carolina in Swain, Jackson and Graham Counties. There are three tracts in the reservation, in the three counties, but the main tract lies in Swain and Jackson counties on the headwaters of the Oconaluftee River. The other tracts, one containing 3200 acres, near Whittier, N. C. is in Swain County and the other tract lies in a remote section of Graham County near the headwaters of the Little and Big Snowbird Rivers.

There are approximately 5000 people on the present Cherokee roll, out of which between seven and eight hundred are full blood. The tribal government recognizes any resident who has one thirty-second part of Cherokee blood. However, by the Cherokee constitution, no member of the tribe can become a council member unless he is of one-quarter blood. He may not be elected Chief unless he is at least half Eastern Cherokee. The council is made up of twelve councilmen; two from each township with the Chief being elected from at large on the Reservation. The council members are elected for two years each, from Paint Town, Wolf Town, Yellowhill, Big Cove, Birdtown and Snowbird townships. These members meet once a year in general council and may meet as many times as necessary at called sessions to settle the business of the tribe. They function as eleven voting members and one President or Speaker of the body. The speaker does not vote except to break a tie.

The Cherokees may lease their lands to outsiders for legitimate purposes up to twenty-five years. All leases must have the approval of the tribal business committee, which is made up of members of the tribal Government and the Superintendent of the Reservation. Although members of the band do not have individual deeds to their lands, they have possessory rights to the tracts they own. These tracts are surveyed and registered in the Federal Agency office, as being held by these individuals. They may swap, trade, or hand down to their legal heirs these tracts of lands and holdings but an heir, to be legal must be at least one thirty-second Cherokee.

The Government maintains one accredited High School and five elementary schools on the Reservation. These schools are operated by the Federal Government under civil service status. Most of the Cherokee students go to these schools but those who wish, and where it is convenient to the local white schools system, go to these schools. It is not mandatory for them to go to Reservation schools.

Cherokees may leave the Reservation at any time and may stay away as long as they desire. They may work where they will and vote in local, county and state elections. The Reservation has its own public health officers and police force. These officers work in conjunction with the local, county and state authorities. Cherokee citizens pay all taxes that ordinary citizens pay except local land taxes. They make their living just as any other Americans do. They do not get a Federal yearly payment, as is the opinion of a great many people.

Some of the older Cherokee people still do not speak English; they may understand the language but refuse to speak it; in fact, only about fifty percent still speak their own language. In the homes, where the older people still speak the language, younger ones learn to speak their own tongue and usually continue to speak it all their lives. The younger people are compelled to learn to speak English in school. The use of the Sequoyah alphabet is fast disappearing. All printing the younger generation comes in contact with is in English. The only time young Cherokees see the Sequoyah alphabet any more, is when the older people sing from their hymn books or read from their Bibles.

Although it is possible to see an Indian ball game occasionally, it is not played any more just for the simple pleasure of maintaining the glory of one's township. The social get-together for the Indian dance is no more. The last of the medicine men are dying and there are no more trained to take their places. Many people do not know the name of their own clan nor the clan of those they marry. The old time Cherokee are fast vanishing and the new generation does not cling to or care for the old ways. They are a part of a different world and look forward to assuming their rightful place in its society.